My Favorite Future

Coloring Book

Written by
Portia Bright Pittman

Illustrated by
Harry Aveira

Dear Reader,
One day, as I watched my first son Derrion explore around the house I began imagining what he would become if only he put his mind to it as he traveled through his youthful years as a kid. This book is meant for you. Take the moment while reading to envision what you want to be and dare to pursue it.
Life is a journey, not a marathon. Never shy away from working to become the greatest version of yourself. You are somebody great and something great is inside of you.
LET'S COLOR!

Sincerely,
DJ & JP'S MOM

My Favorite Future

Identifiers:
ISBN (Paperback) 978-1-7349356-7-7

WRITE YOUR NAME BELOW AND SPEAK THE CHANT ALOUD.

My name is ___________________________ and I am somebody great. My dreams matter. I am bright, bold and gifted. My dreams matter. I shall be what I put my mind and hard work into becoming. My future does matter! I am destined to become something and someone great. Watch me work!

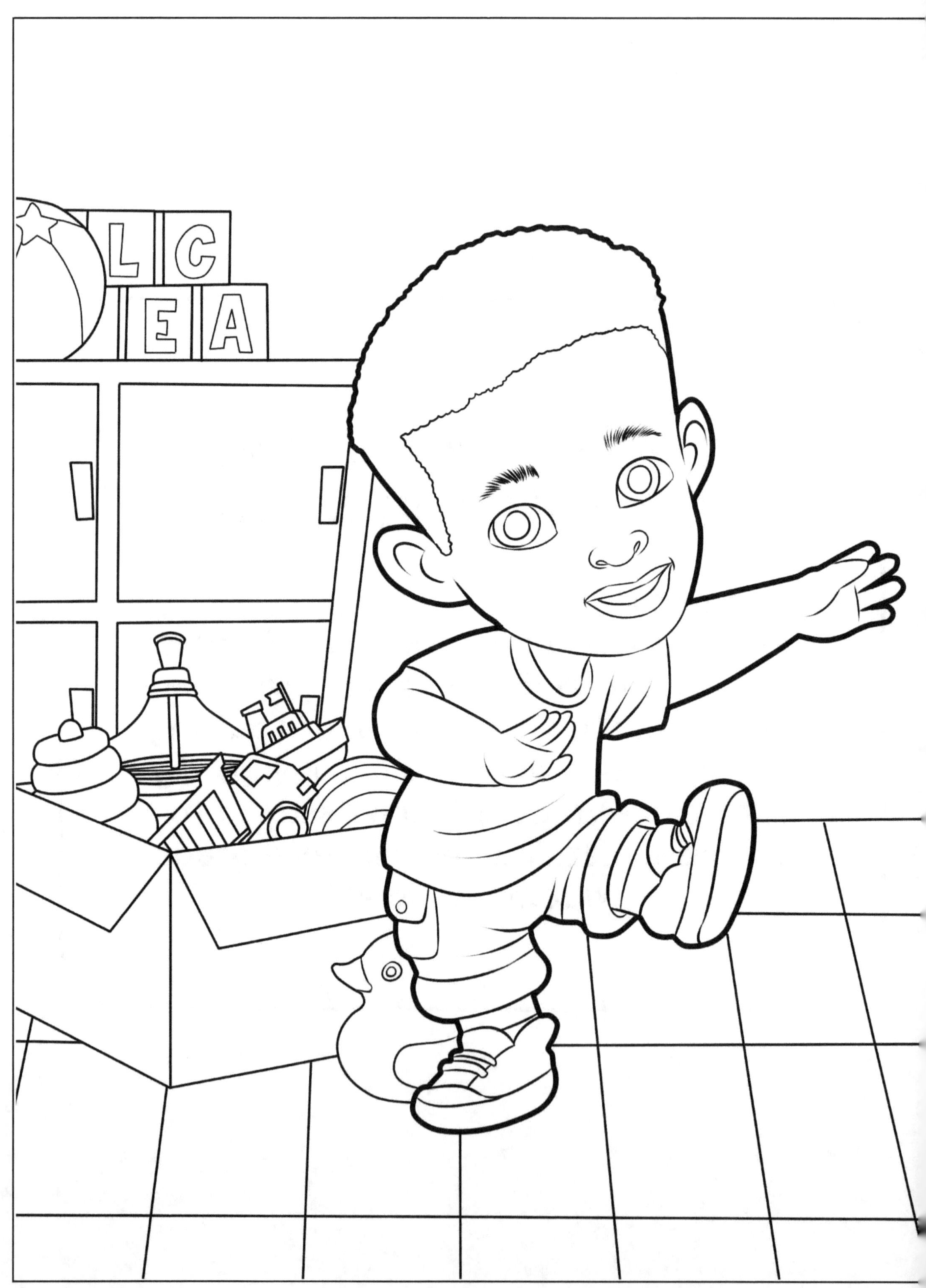
L C
E A

BE KIND

TO EVERY KIND

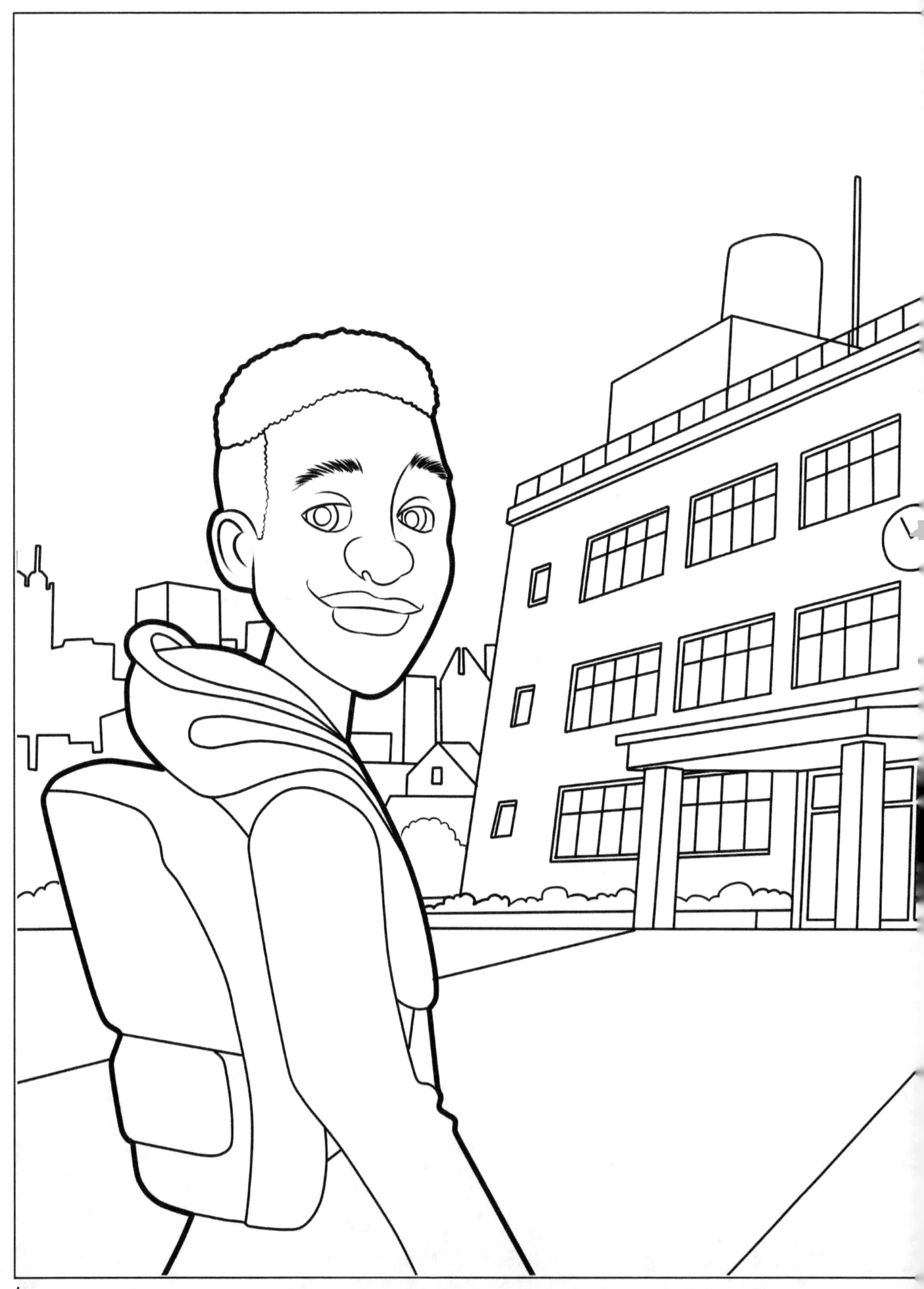

DREAM FOR IT

AND THEN

WORK

TOWARDS

IT

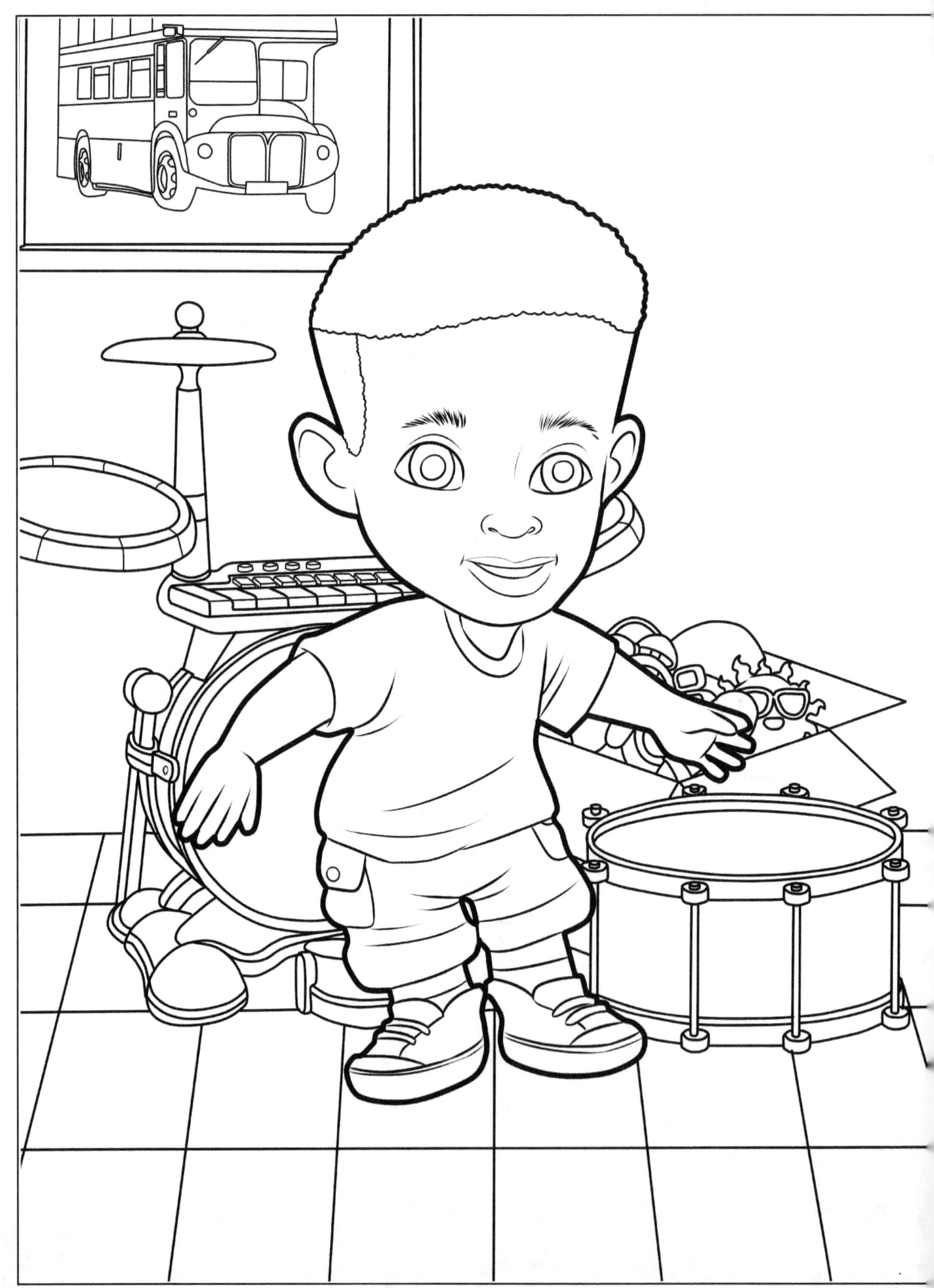

I AM SOMEBODY TO BELIEVE IN

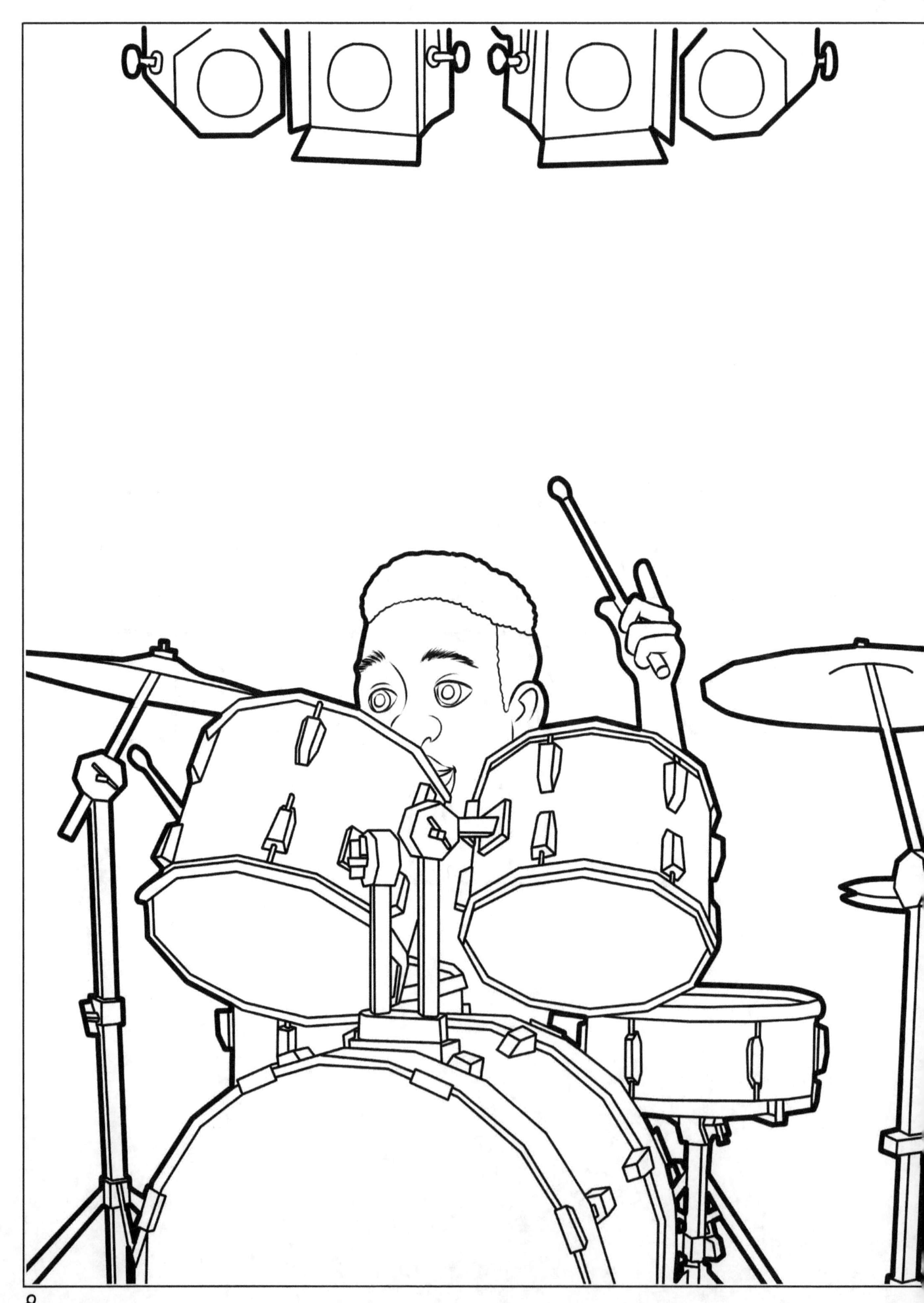

DO SOMETHING TODAY

THAT YOUR FUTURE SELF CAN SAY "OH YEAH THAT ROCK'S"!

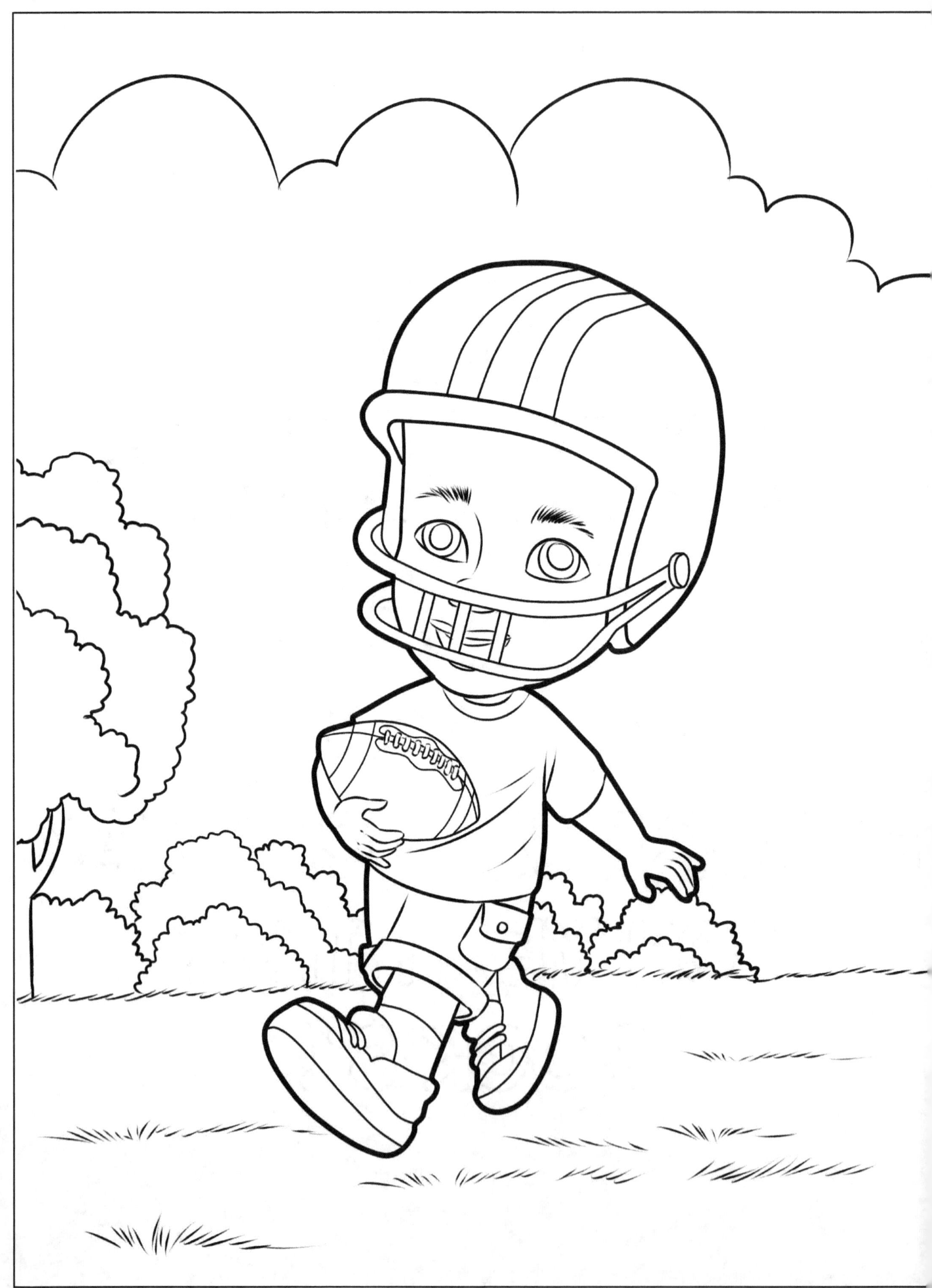

IF YOU WANT TO

SEE A BRIGHTER FUTURE AHEAD

YOU HAVE TO START WORKING TOWARDS A GOAL TODAY

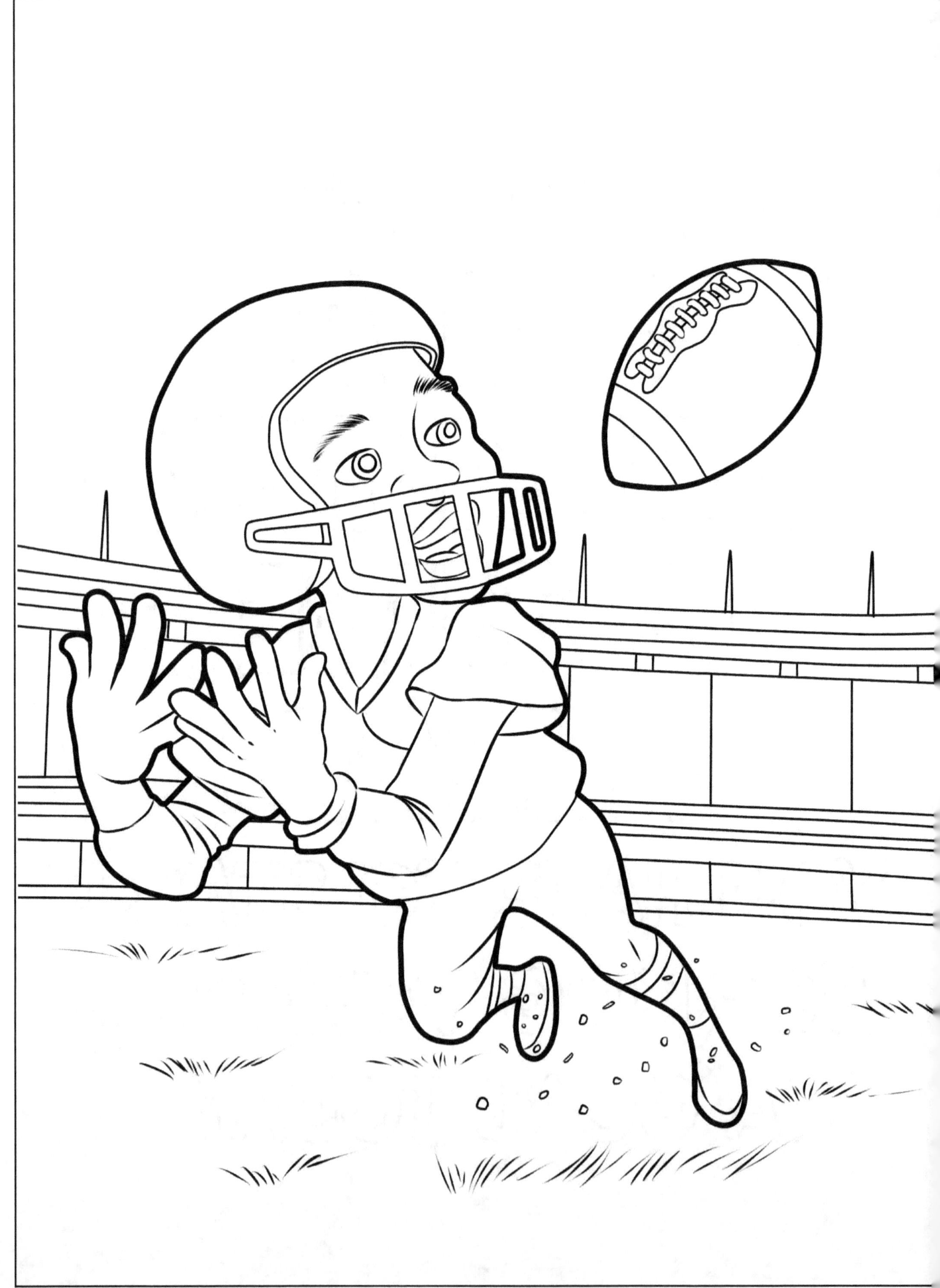

BREATHE & HAVE PATIENCE

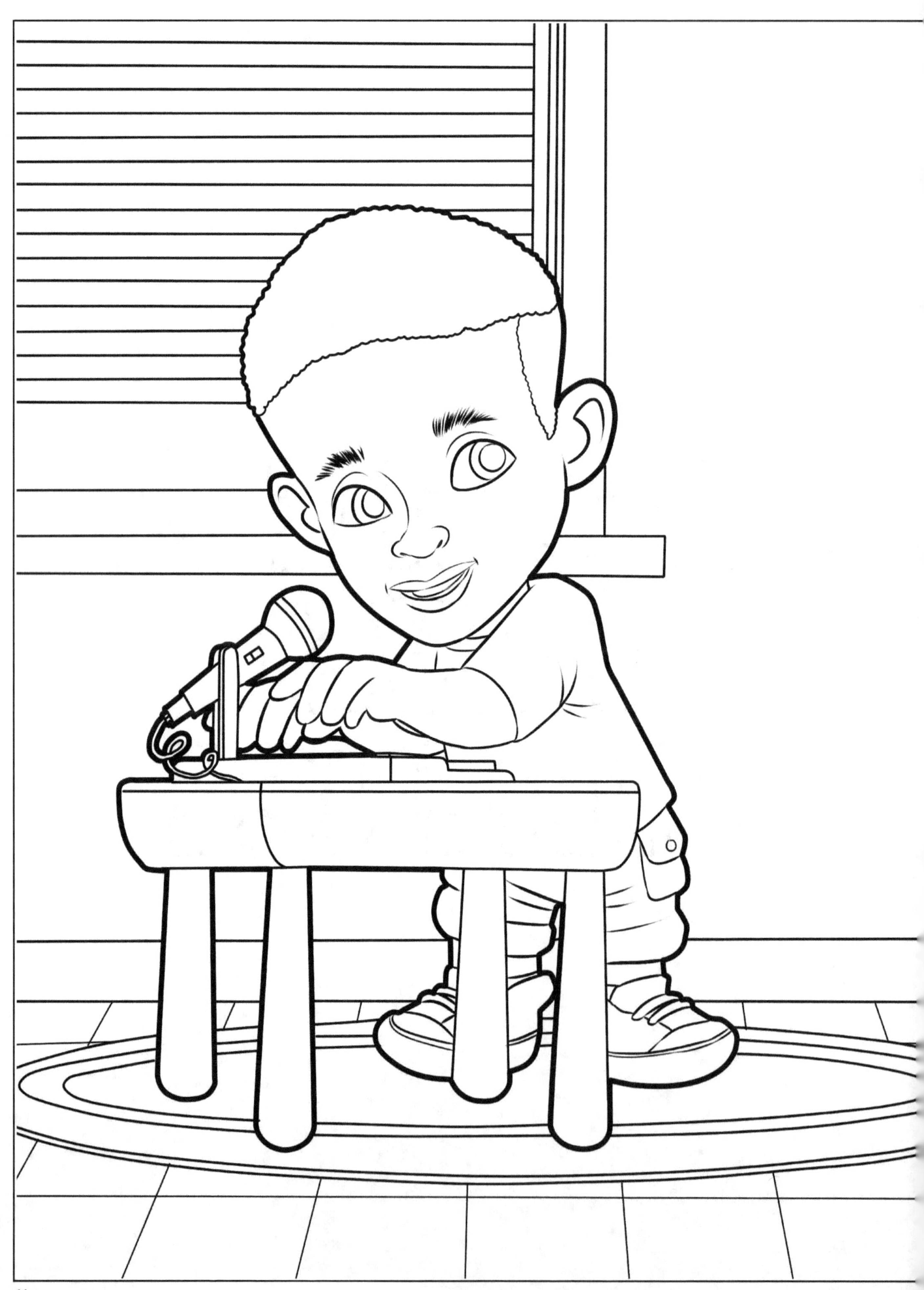

BELIEVE

THERE IS A
BRIGHTER FUTURE
AHEAD OF YOU

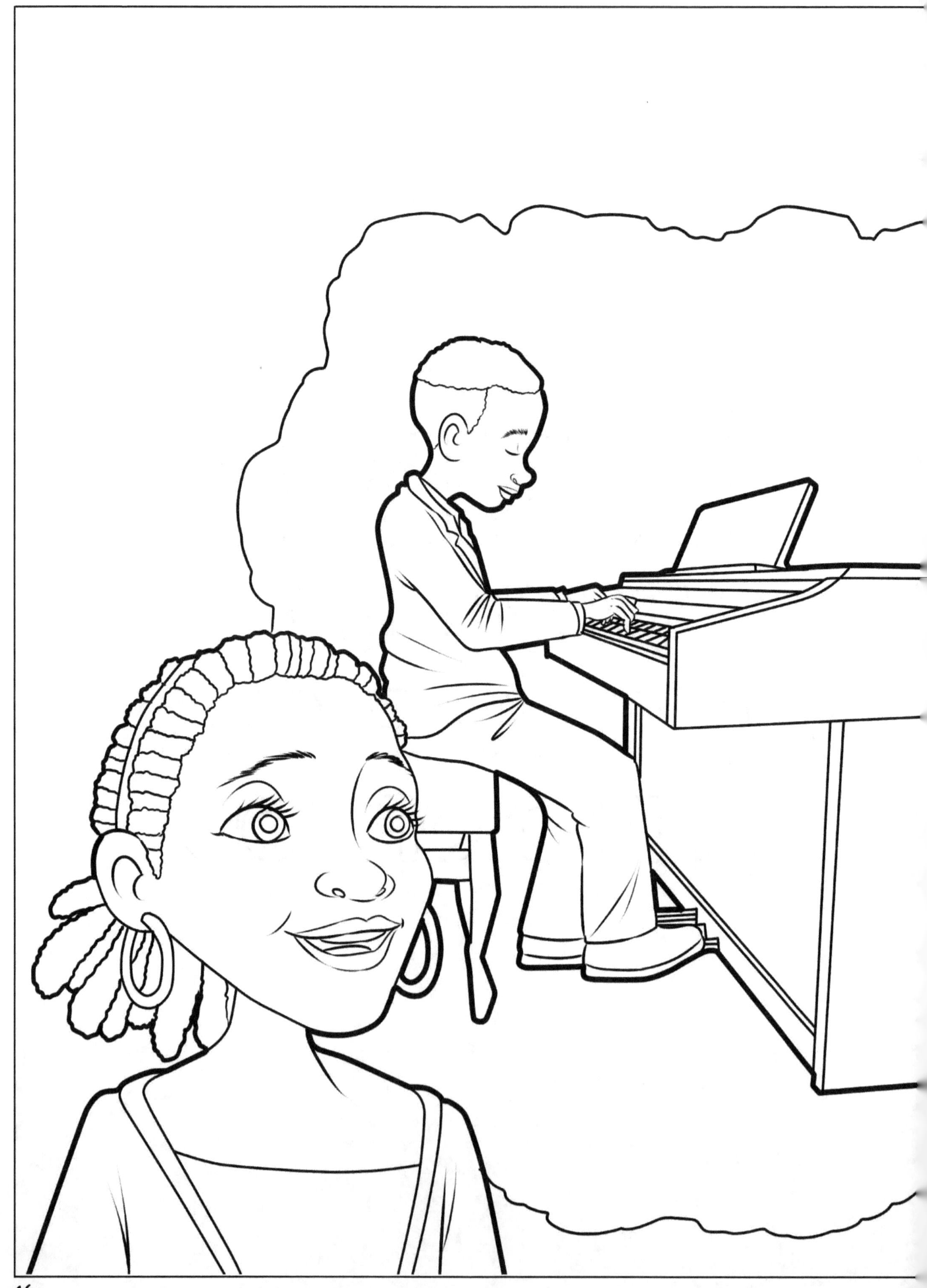

YOUR

DREAMS

CANT PLAY A PART
IN YOUR FUTURE
UNLESS YOU MAKE
THEM COME TRUE

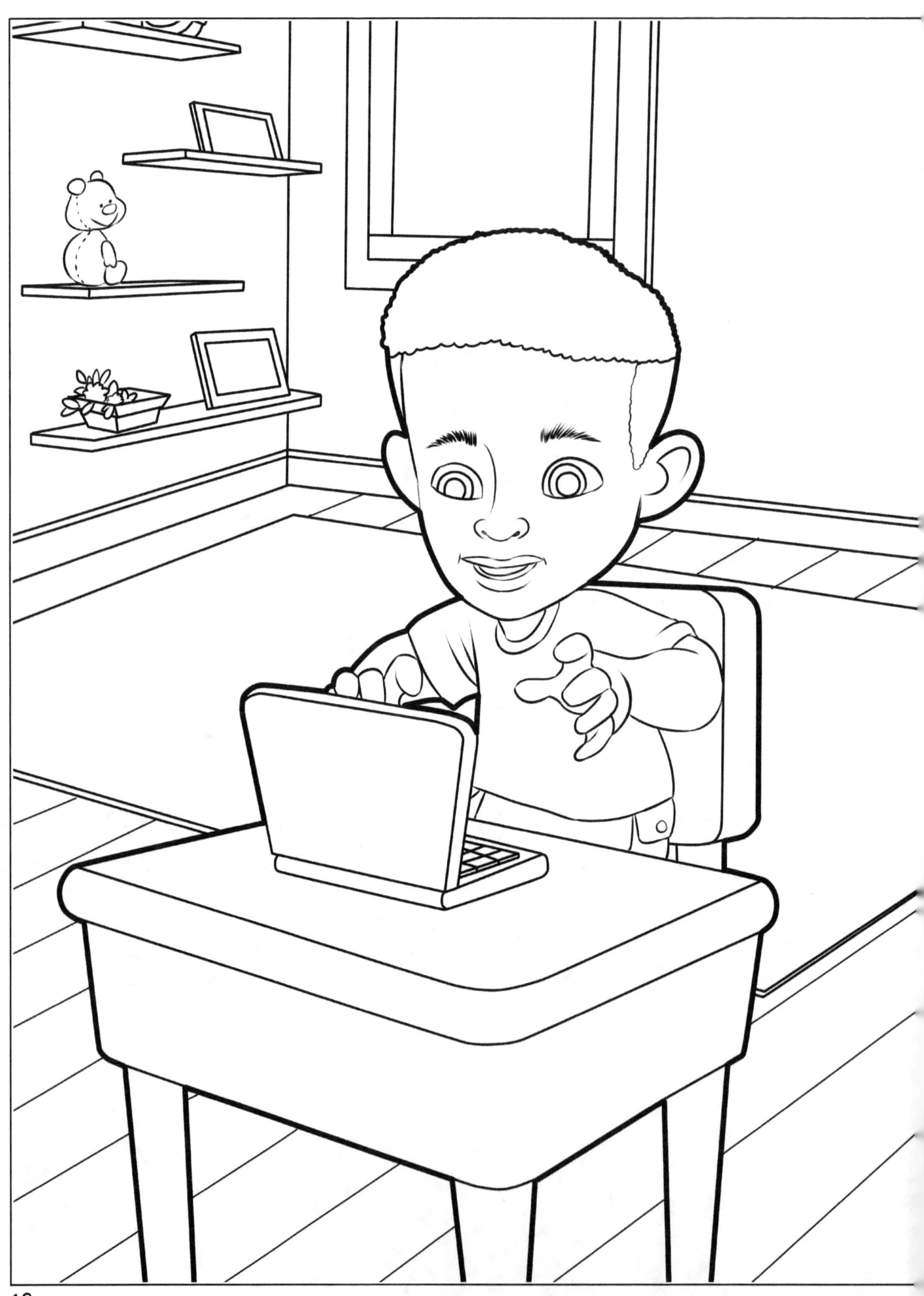

NEVER GIVE UP ON YOU

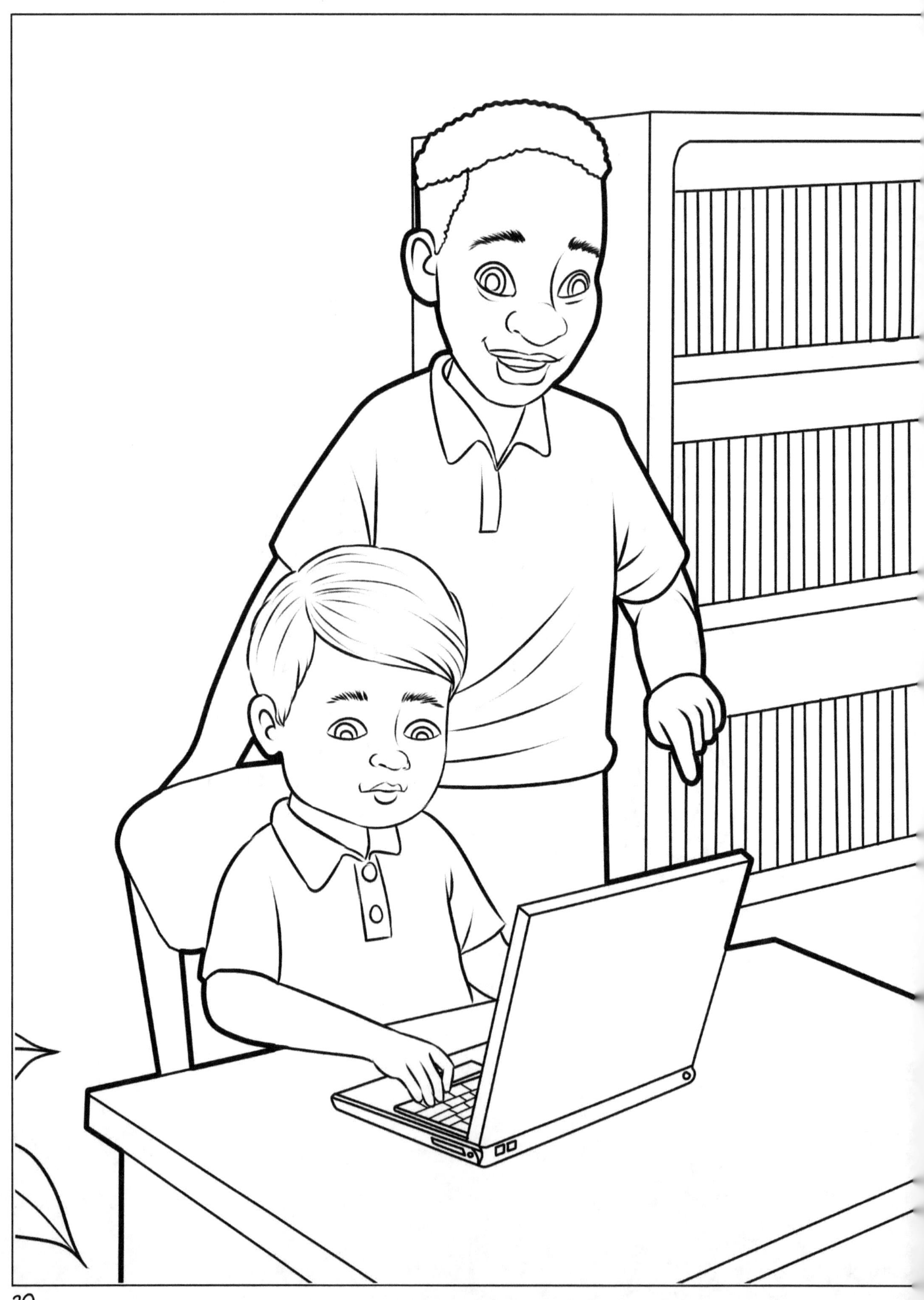

IF LIFE HURTS

TALK TO SOMEONE ABOUT IT

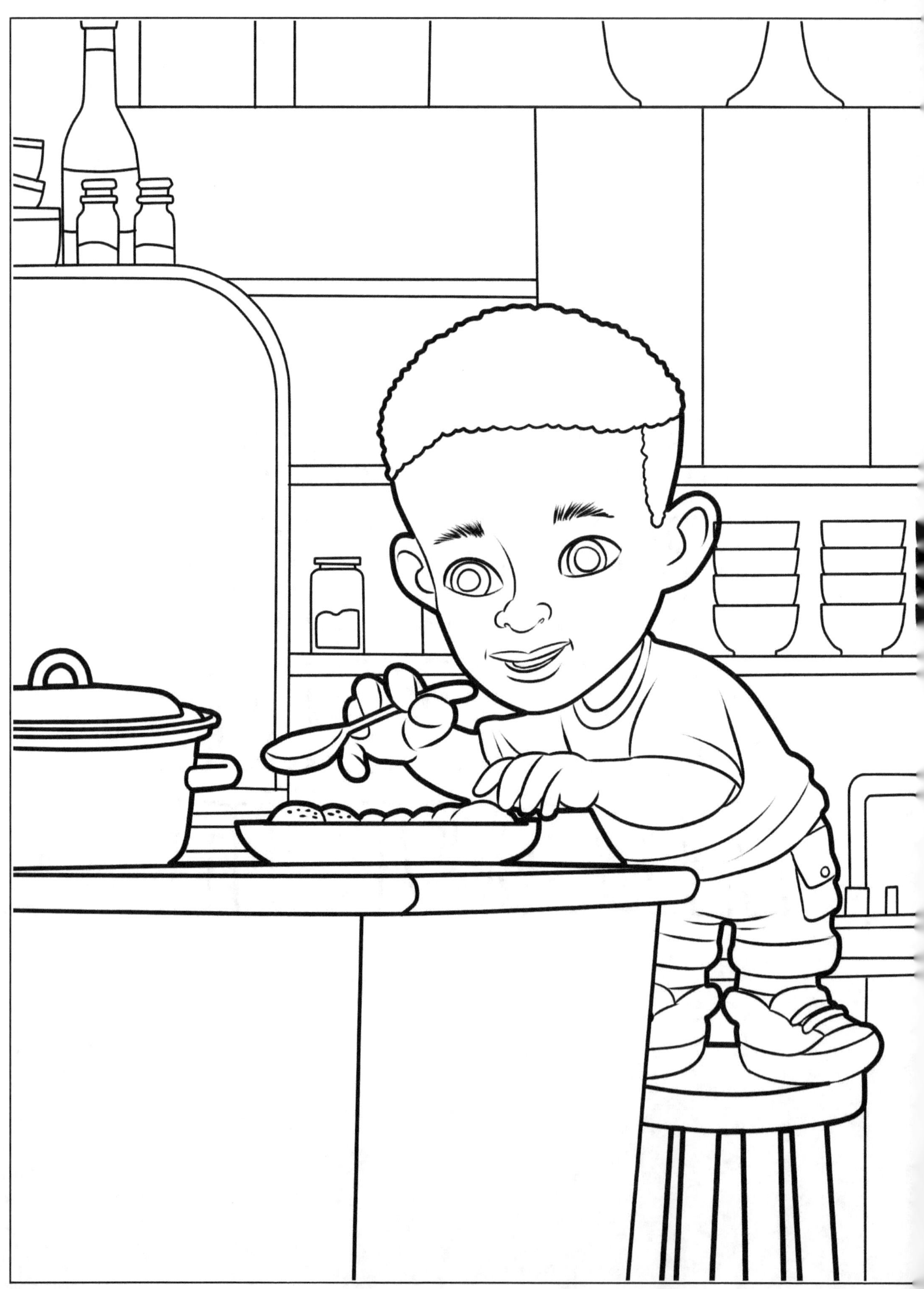

ALWAYS HAVE THE

COURAGE

TO TRY

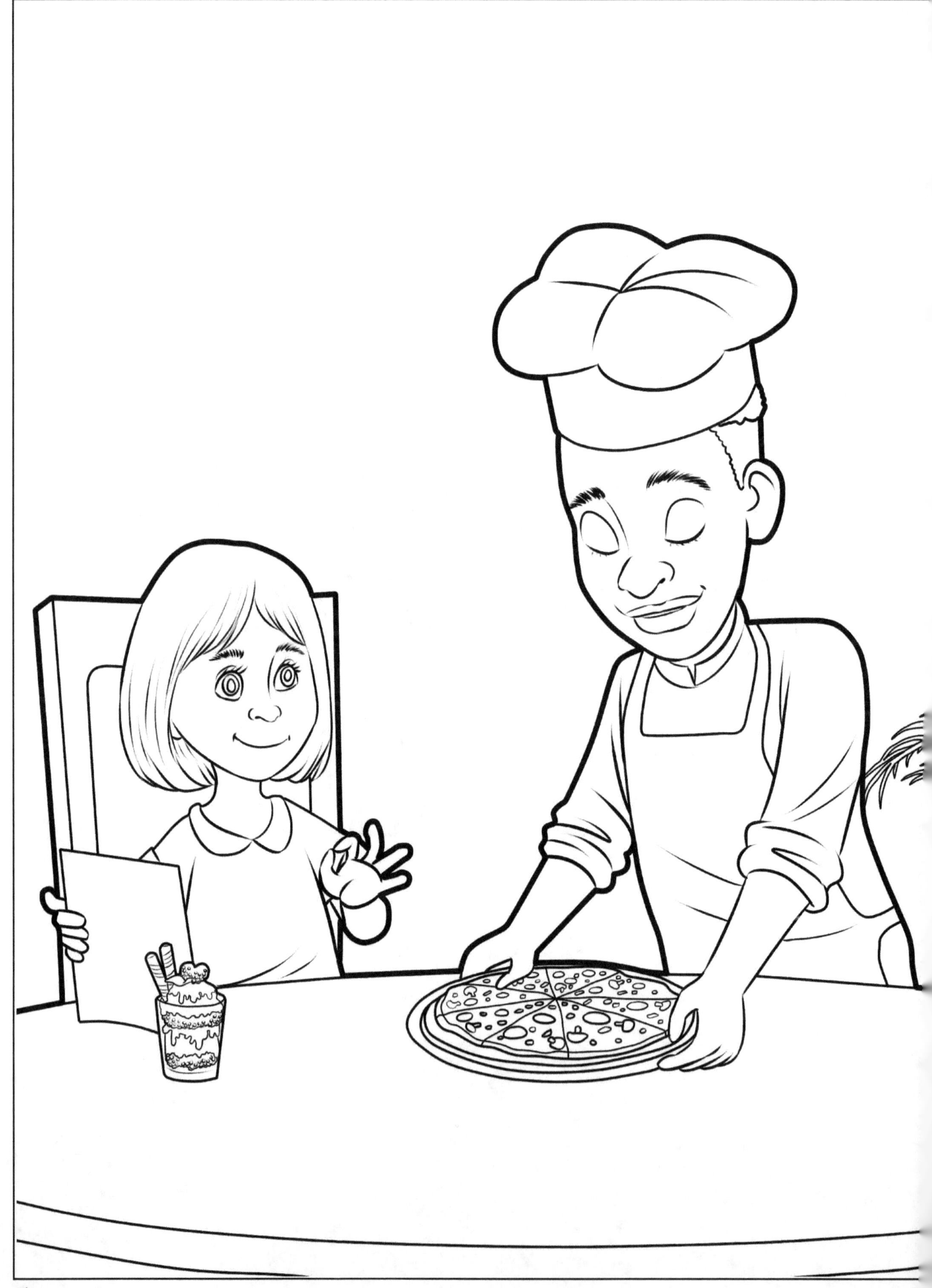

BE INSPIRING

ALWAYS HAVE A SPIRIT OF GRATITUDE

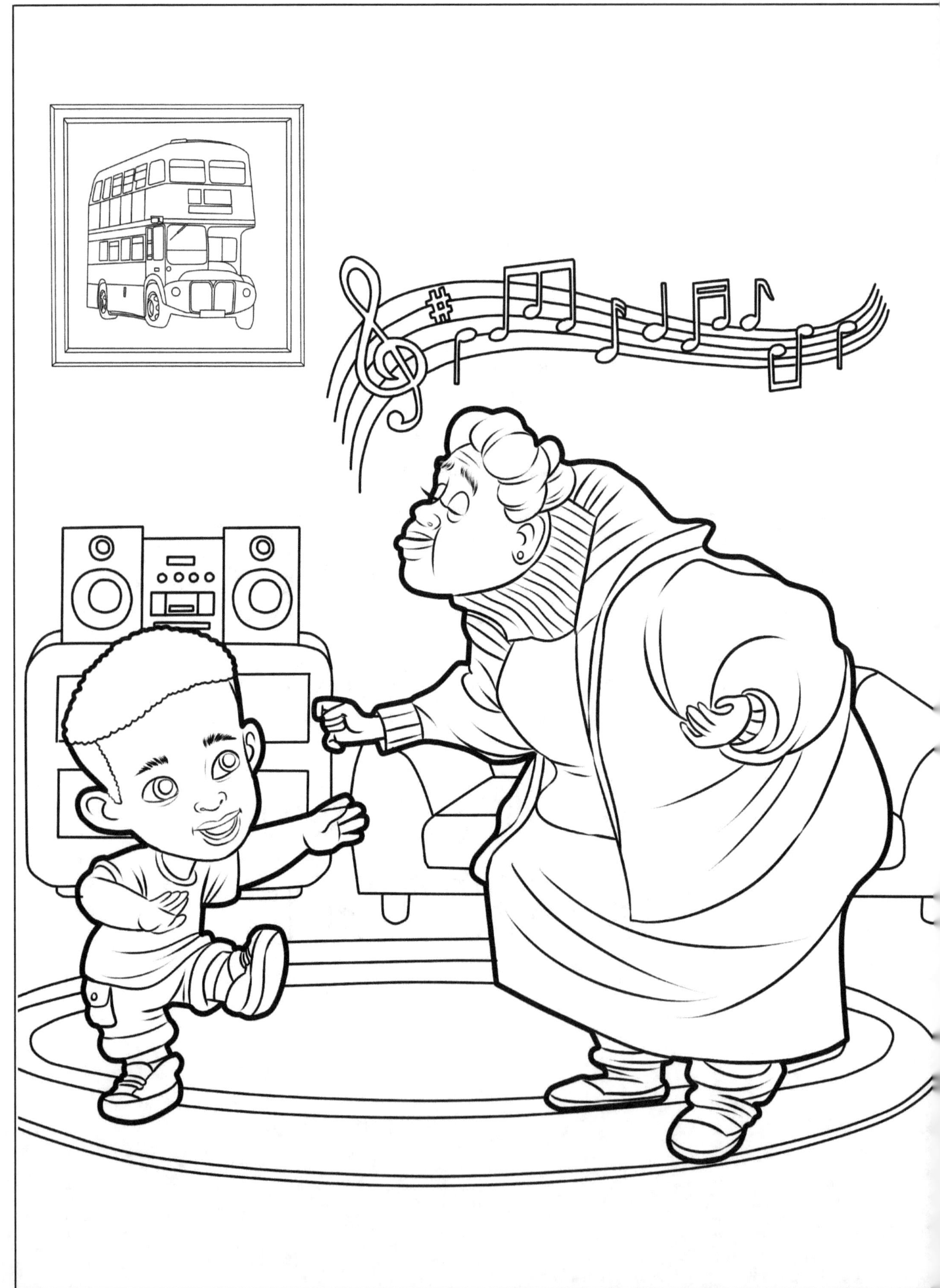

APPRECIATE THE TIME YOU SPEND WITH LOVED ONE'S

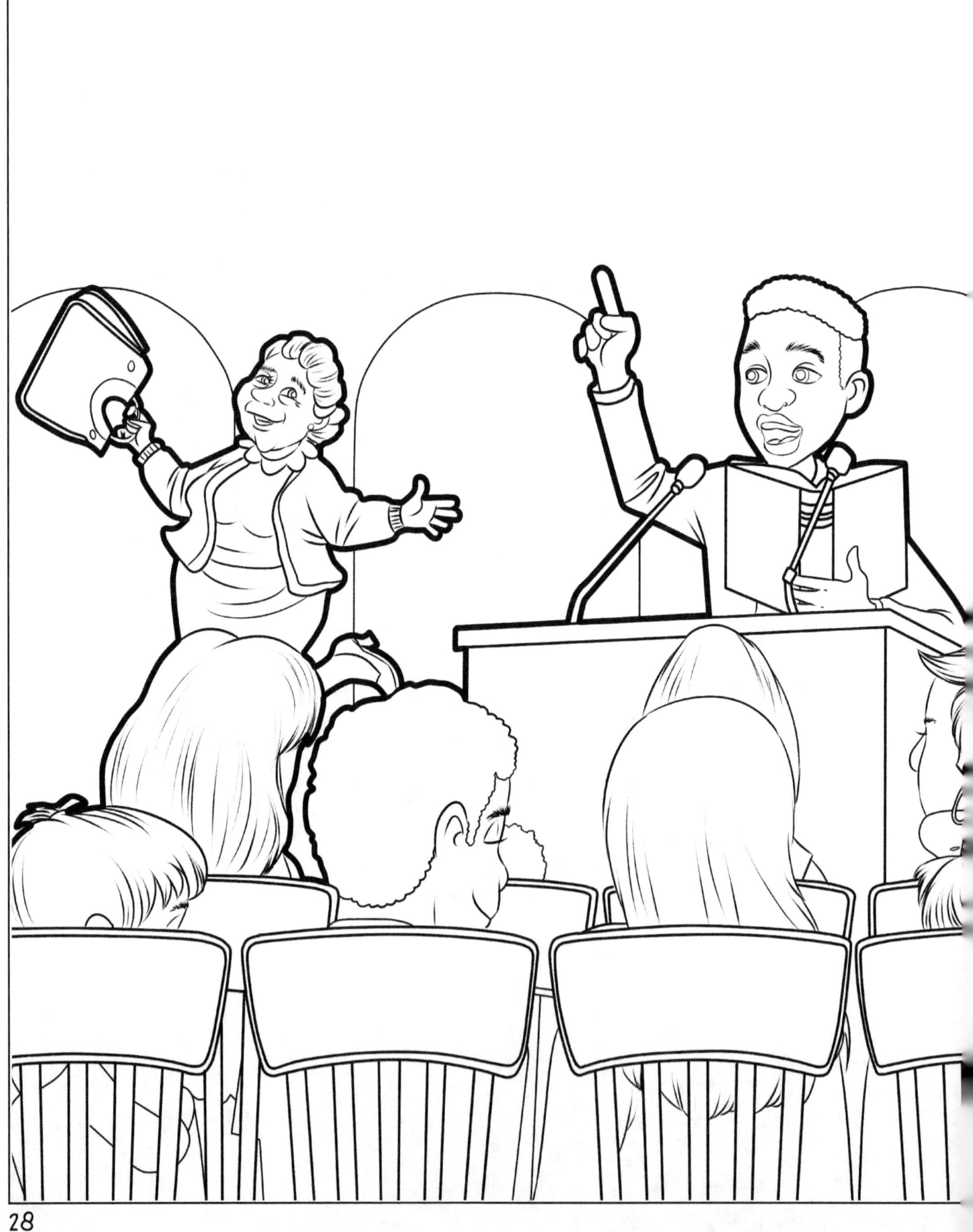

SPEAK YOUR TRUTH, BE INSPIRATIONAL, AND PUSH TOWARDS INSPIRING OTHER'S

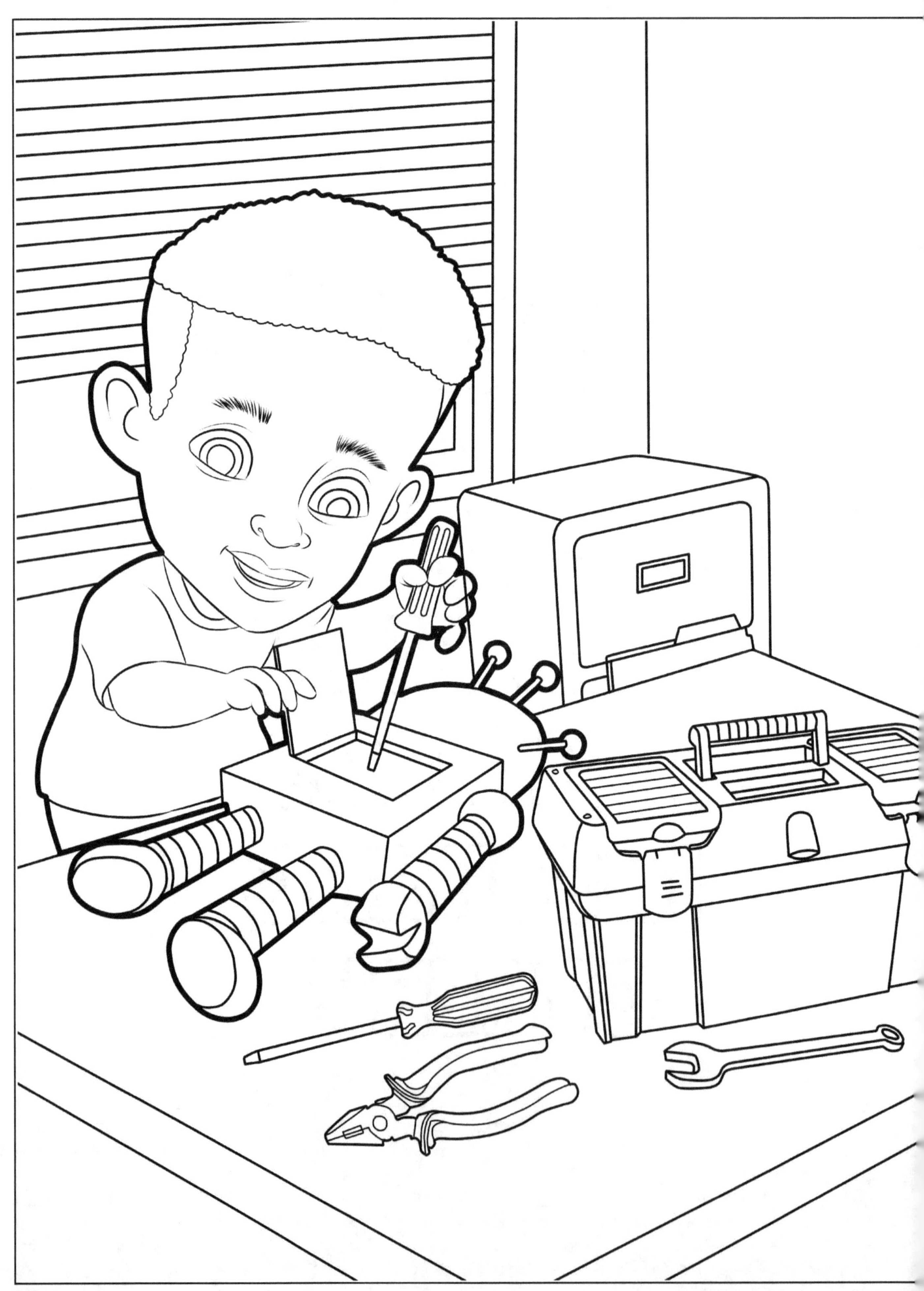

THINKING OUTSIDE THE BOX CAN HELP YOU FIND THE RIGHT SOLUTION

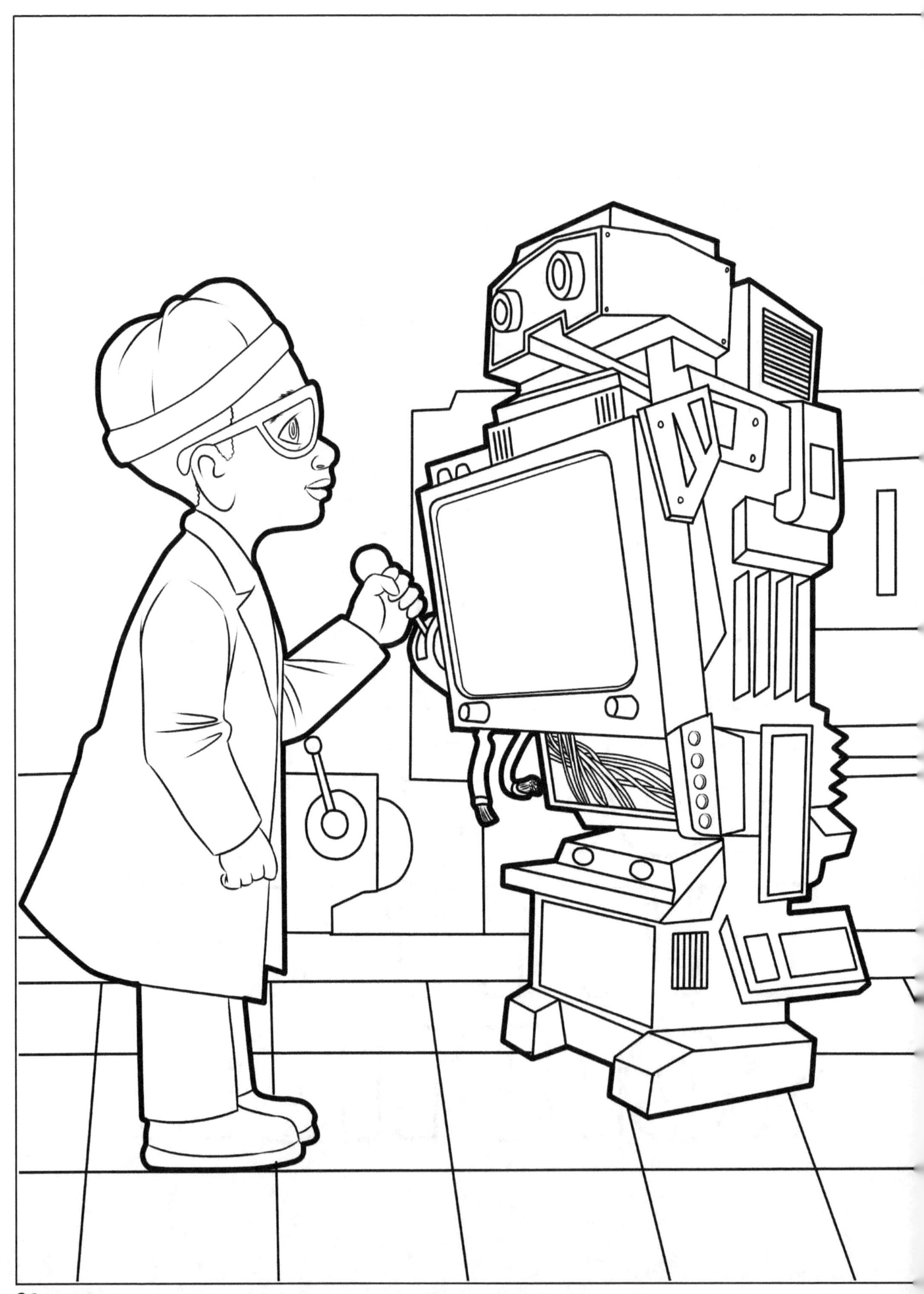

CREATING YOUR OWN PATH CAN HELP BUILD A BETTER FUTURE

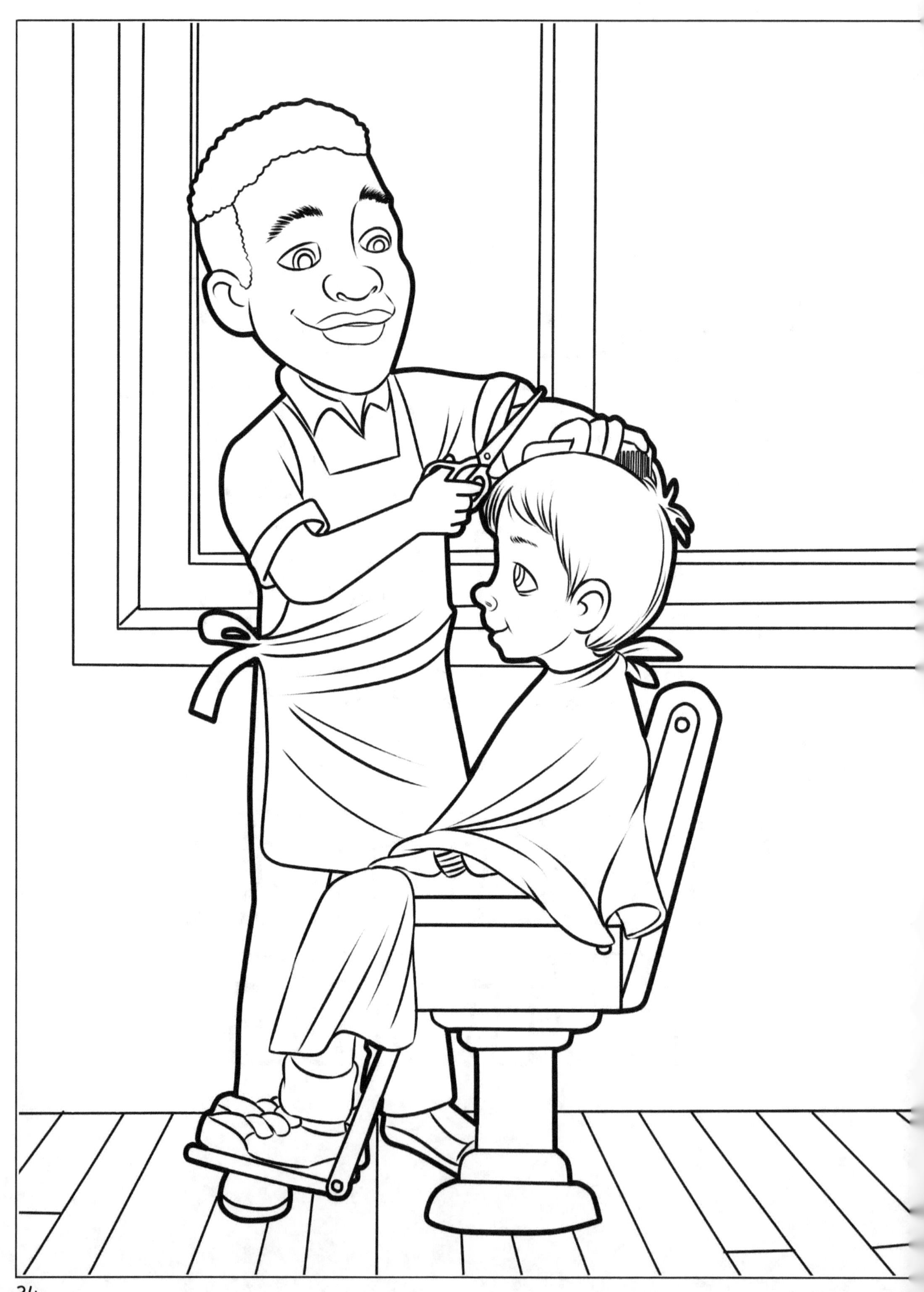

BE A CUT ABOVE THE REST

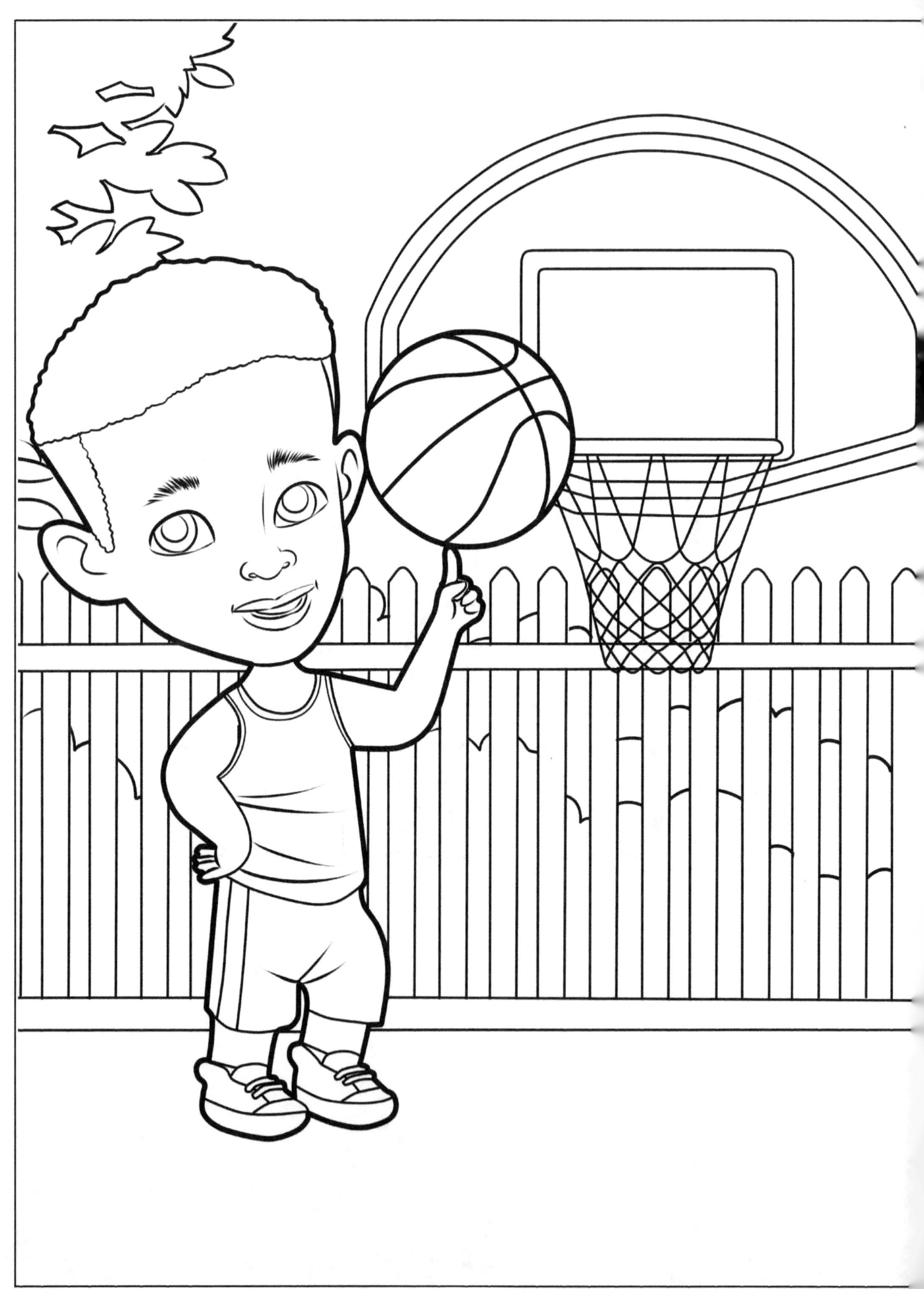

YOU ARE A GAME CHANGER

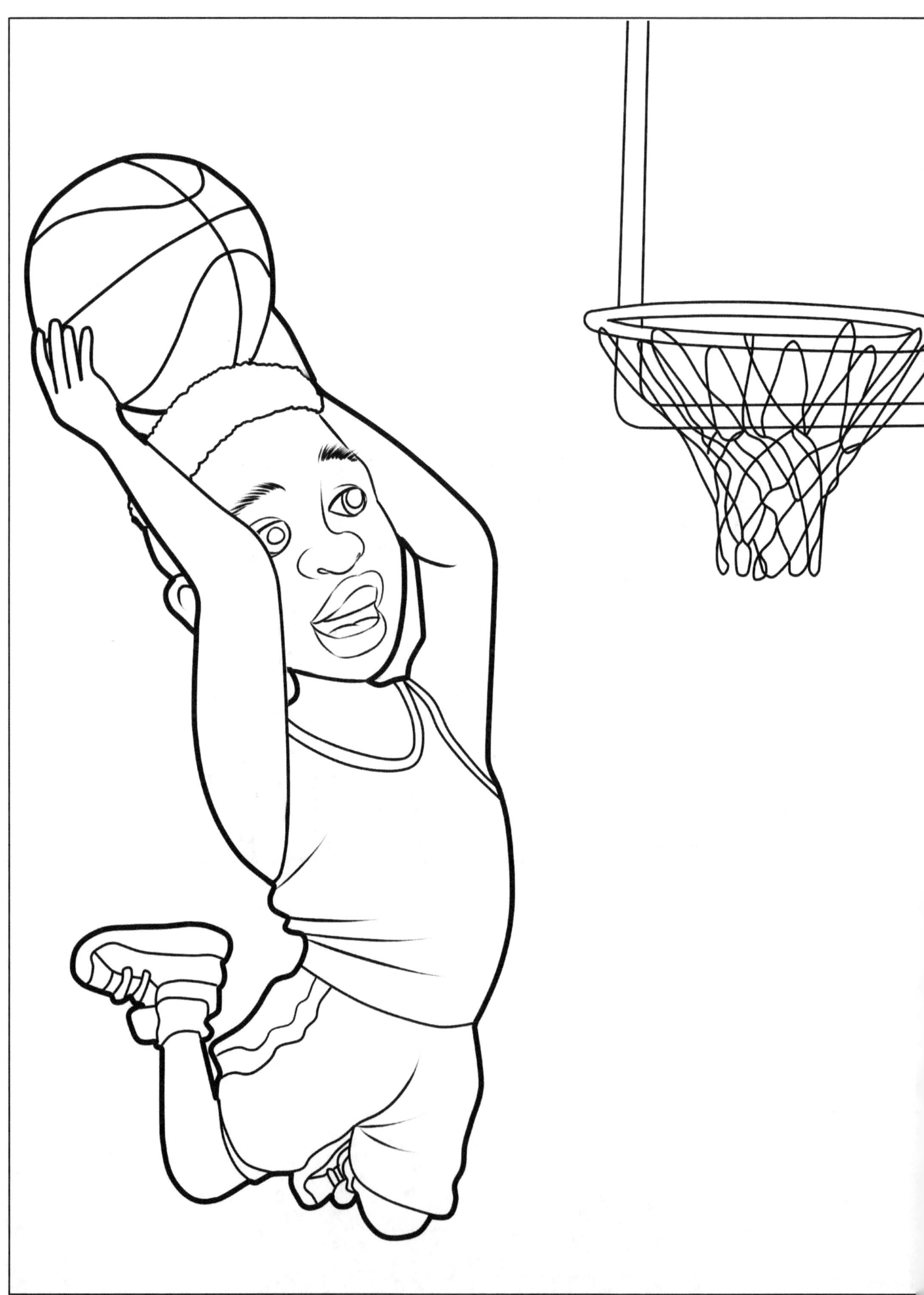

SET A GOAL THEN AIM HIGH

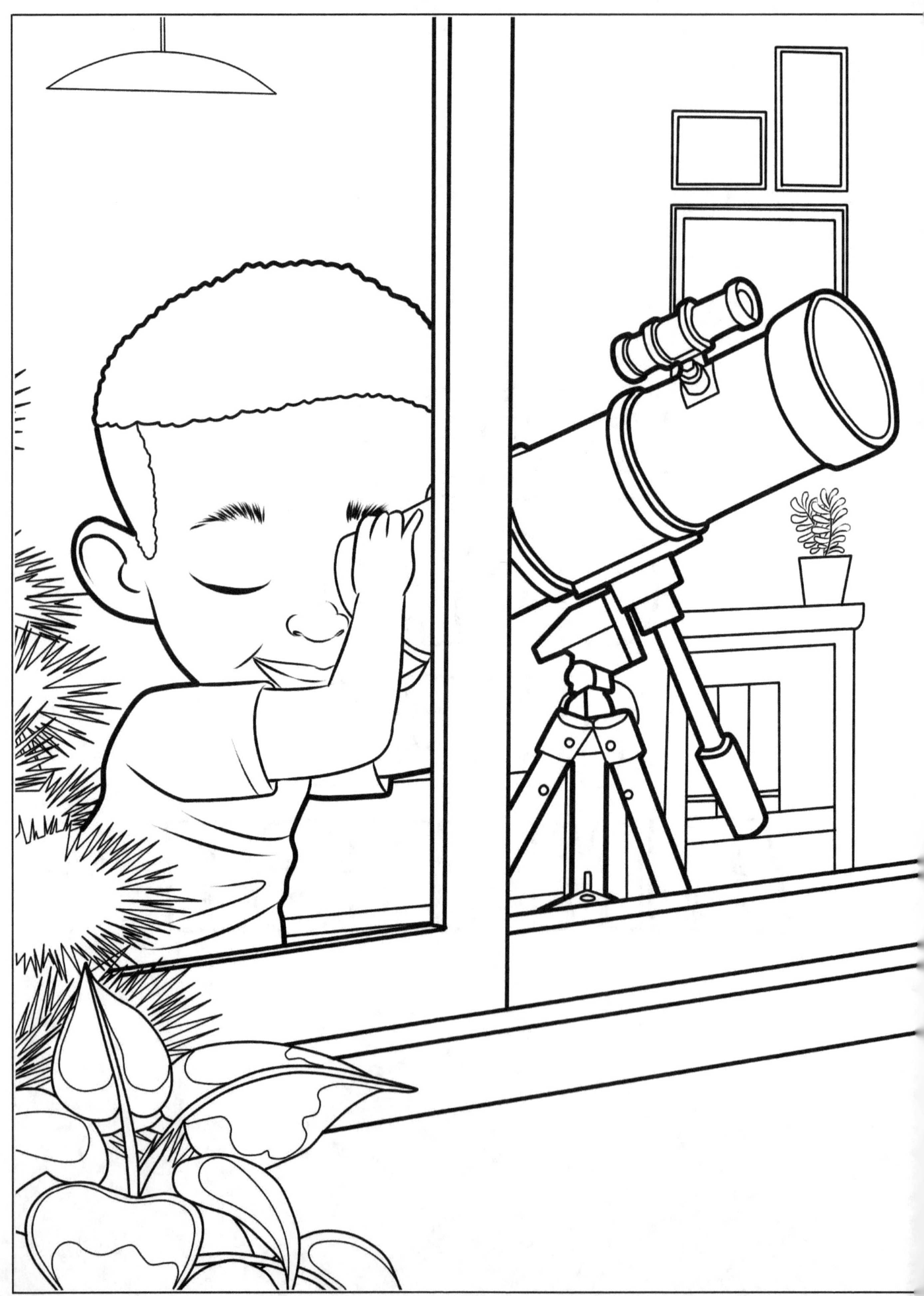

AIM HIGH
TO REACH
THE STARS

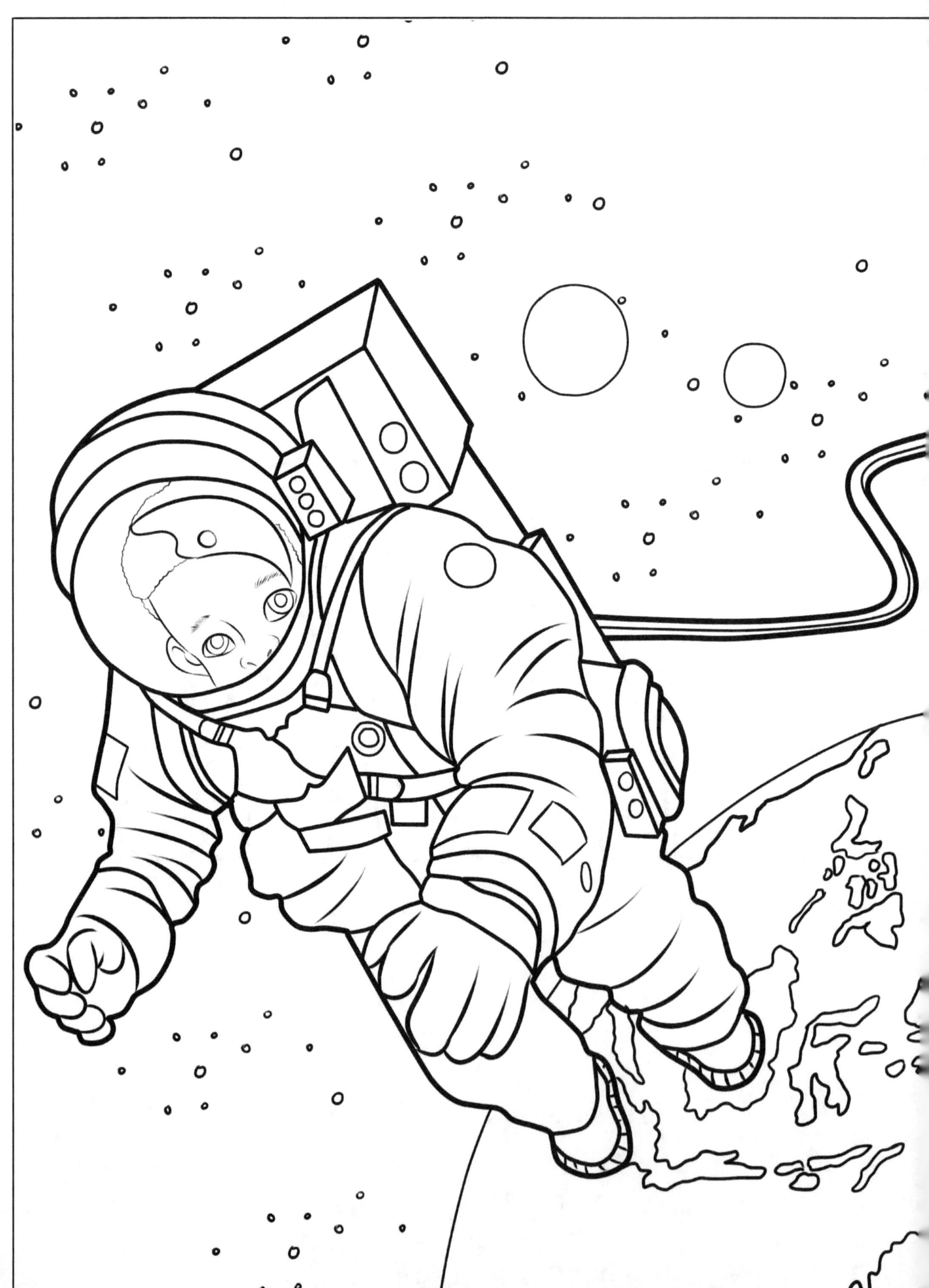

REACH BEYOND THE STARS

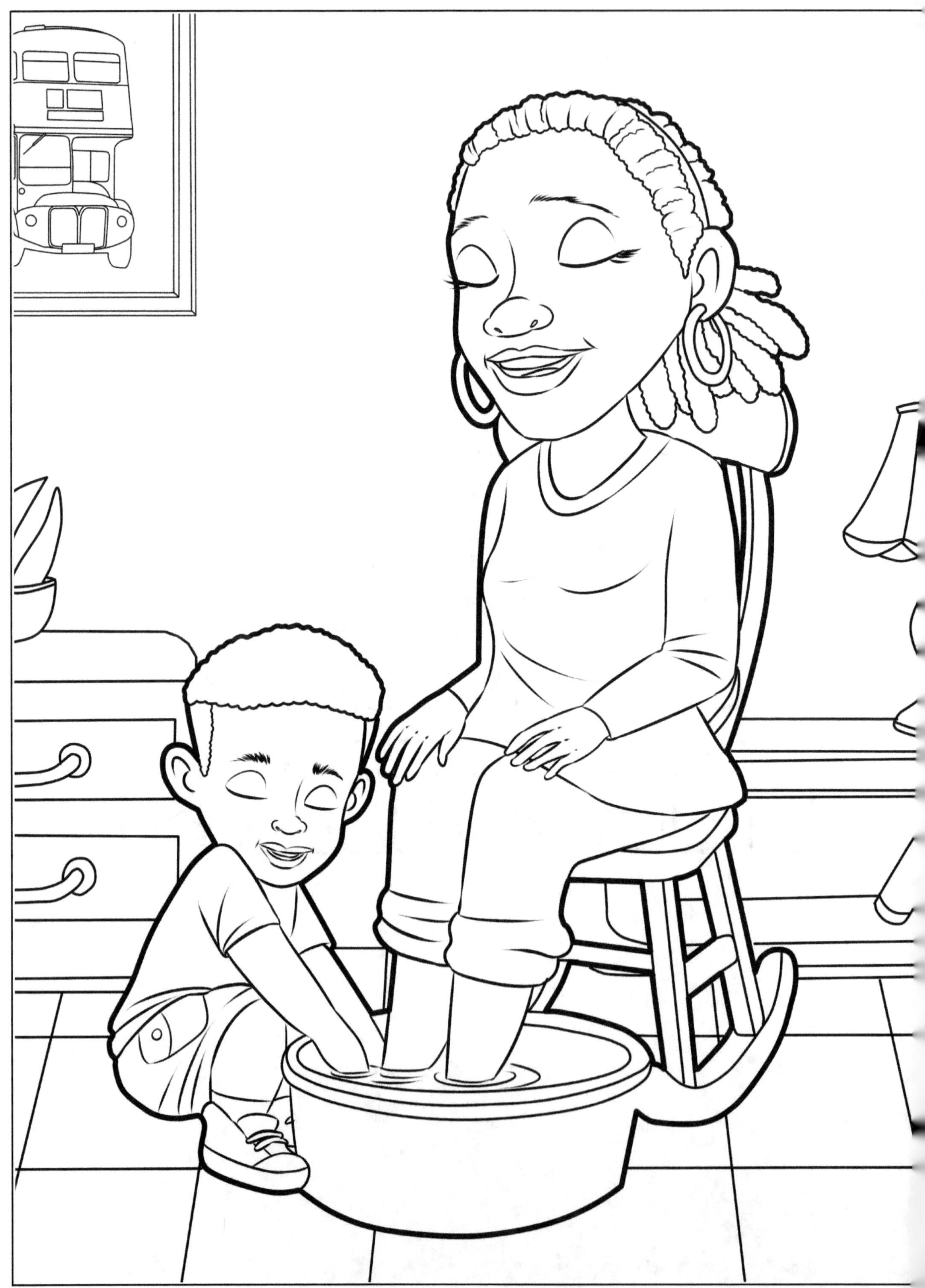

RESPECT THOSE AROUND YOU BUT MOST IMPORTANTLY ALWAYS RESPECT YOUR ELDERS

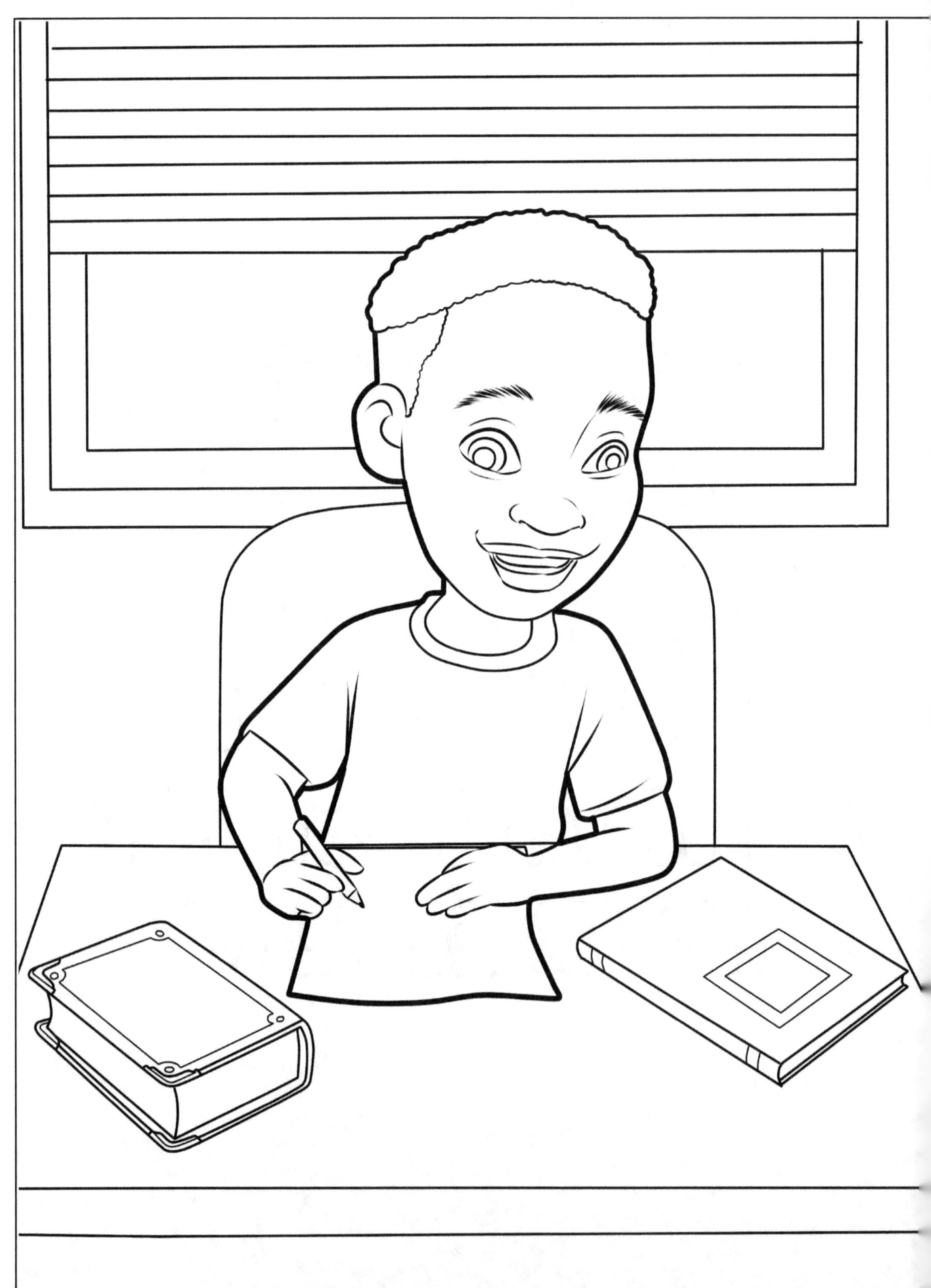

READING IS A SUPERPOWER THAT WILL HELP YOU BECOME YOUR BEST SELF!

DREAM LOG

DREAM LOG

DREAM LOG

DREAM LOG

DREAM LOG

Thank You!

Please continue to follow the journey by subscribing to our youtube channel, facebook, instragram and tiktok @brightbooksclub

Visit our website at www.brightbooks.org

www.ingramcontent.com/pod-product-compliance
Lightning Source LLC
LaVergne TN
LVHW061257100826
845148LV00008B/1154
* 9 7 8 1 7 3 4 9 3 5 6 7 7 *